Special edition anthology

hashtag #not_ashamed

Let's grow and bloom together

First Published in September 2020

ISBN: 978-81-947634-9-9

Price: 199₹

Author & Proof Reading: Komal R.

Distributed by-

Paperback: Flipkart (India), Amazon.com (US, UK, DE, FR, ES, IT, JP)
E-Book: Amazon, Apple (iBooks stores in 51 countries), Barnes & Noble (US and UK), Scribd, Kobo, and Blio, OverDrive (world's largest library ebook platform serving 20,000+ libraries), Baker & Taylor Axis 360, Tolino, Gardners (Askews & Holts and Browns Books for Students), Bibliotheca Cloud Library (3,000 public libraries) and Odilo (2,100 public libraries in North America, South America and Europe) + Paperback

What is #not_ashamed?

Hashtag #not_ashamed is about promoting mental health awareness, where we want to break stereotypes among people of mental issues. Some small things often cause big issues and we want to break it.

Let's stop pretending that we are okay when we are not!

"We are not ashamed to tell that we are going through some serious sht right now."**

hashtag
#not_ashamed

Suchismita Ghoshal

This is Suchismita Ghoshal from West bengal, India.Her schooling was completed from Barlow Girls High School in Malda.She is 21 & pursuing her graduation in Zoology in Malda College.

She has always been a curious soul from childhood & used to observe things intensely .

She belongs from a small town but her dreams are to touch the sky keeping her feet to the ground.

She loves to read ponderous amount of books & this left an impact on writing by her own.She's been in this profession for 4 years & loves to write poetry, short story & anything inspires her.She enhances her writing skill by feeling each & every incident through her heart.She has been a published co-author of more than 20 anthologies till now.She loves travelling & gaining knowledge beside writing.She is keen to photoshoots & a freelance model & loves acting on theatres.

She aspires to be a good author as well as a book reviewer in near future.

I AM NOT ASHAMED

Flipping through the pages of my life, i stumbled upon on every chapters where i faced hurdles at a different age of a different day on a different time.They always bombard scavenging the rest of the garbages from the floor of my heart.

I never spend a day without drooling tear drops, & wilderness of their pain.

Days are tasteless salads & nights feel like an almost blackened piece of a roasted chicken, bitter & neutralizes my tastebuds.

Let's make a prompt travel through the choked alleys of my life & pick some selective pictures to prepare a catalogue.

At the age of 3-

Childhood are gold wrapped with silver cellophane papers,i heard somewhere.But why didn't i match it like that way? Why do i miscalculate the measurements every time.Because, it was neither illuminated with gold, nor with silver , it only was blackened with dark & intense jelly of problems & i got glued in them badly.Shrieks from every nook & corner, still directly hit my ears until it bleeds. Unending conflicts between my parents still climb through the cracked wall of heart & cut it into pieces.Dolls seem angry & broken as i never got time to play & sing with them.I cried, i continued sobbing fearfully....

At the age of 7-

Neither the conflicts came to an end, nor the intentions behind it named any resolution rather than increasing with the tick-tocking of wall clock.One more added in the consequence to concatenate my scars more;my class teacher complained about my inattentiveness & intentional scattered strokes of pen in my notebook instead of a bunch of solved sums.They only saw a girl stay quiet, didn't bother to solve her inner inequations ,which slowly ate her to the core.I was scolded by my mother, her teardrops again drenched my soul, i took oath to carry a burden on my shoulder, i stood between 3rd rank every year from then! Remember that i didn't stop crying, i still carried on.......

At the age of 10-

I was a meritorious student now, with my attires odoured like a exceptional polymath, other children of my age used to love my company, & i used to get curious.Probably my immature brain wasn't enough to articulate the selfish gestures of them.Well, my father now was a prey of neuro-psychiatric problem.He remained reckless, overhasty & anxiety ridden always.

My mother stressed a lot, & pictures of a rushing life flashed upon in front of my eyes & promptly changed, then the next day came same like this & also passed, the cycle of unstable life continually poked on the deepest point of my brain.Wait, i didn't stop studying hard, my mom dictated each time crying, " You have to brighten up our face & shine out overcoming this problems!"

The only way to ignite with hues of colours were to embrace those neuter books, notebooks,pens & pencils & i followed my duty to see her happy.I forgot i was slowly losing my childhood skies, i sighed, i missed those green meadows.Sometimes i weeped, i weeped in glooms of loss....

At the age of 11-

I felt i was changing slowly,my chest wasn't flat like before, it was growing a little bit, i didn't either looked bad, & pre-pubescent days of my life noticed the transformation of my thighs, my tender & smooth skin of light complexion.But one day, i knew i wasn't that small to be mercied from the tongues painted lusts when a worker in our home touched my thighs with a small effort of squeezing it & my frightened soul ran scribbling some of my messy & nauseous thoughts randomly escaping from his greedy grip.I remained quiet, locked in my room, mirrors were bad now ,i didn't like the mirage of my body.I visualized the pair of hands slowly grabbing me in the goblet of forbidden lust , though i consoled my soul saying , “Maybe, uncles do this things playfully.It doesn’t matter if it felt way too worse than anything.” I wish i were acknowledged then with the facts of new channels’ headlines like , “ a 10 year old girl is raped in her school”! I still cried for that day, with all my numb senses,& murky being i sobbed piercing my soul....

At the age of 13-

“Friendships are made from the heaven.

Friends are the guides of your life.

Friends enlightens your way of thinking....”

Such punchlines now got revealed in front of my eyes in a broad daylight.I forgot to mention, i had a best friend whom i missed from closing my heavy lidded eyes at night to opening the lashes of my eyes in morning.She seemed like an unsung lullabies to my ears, surreal to my eyes & inarticulate notion to my lips.

But the reality cooked something else for my burnt fate, our sections changed, she transferred from “B” to “D” section & i stayed stagnant there.Colorful tiffin breaks now painted a grey & feeble portrait of colorless days,tinted with only glooms.I used to shed my ears for our separation & all of sudden was rewarded with a sweet gesture from her, she labelled it with “All drama”.

My world fell apart, still i gathered to stand up with my bruised knees & fragmented bones.I smiled suppressing the leaked flows of my remorse, they flooded me merging.I set her free, let her go as i started believing the universe is a dramatized stage where everyone comes to show their part & leave fast. I whimpered fetching the broken pieces of my being....

At the age of 14-

Now my face was covered with the dots of pimples, just when i slightly touched the borders of “ adolescence”, they bumped,started lining up on my skin.Still then, i was unsatisfied, but now, i cursed my skin more than anything, crushing those little monsters but they had the powers of Ravana's heads, i squeezed them & they again incarnated.Till now, their storyline went well but from the very fast day, when i was alleged with unnecessary teases like , “She has a very rough skin.Look at her pimps!” & list doesn’t end here as my goggling collar bone, lean wrist & wide waist too offended my peers’ mind & peeled off their layers of peace.Now, i hated going school, avoided my tuitions to escape those shitty bullies.I searched for a dollop of peace in between the widely nourished pests of this society.I started assuming the only way to survive in this narrow passage of earth to look better & have a smooth toned epidermis in your whole body, scarless & doped with articificiality.I howled a lot, a lot in this trepidation of human traps....

At the age of 16-

Hormone games triggered my emotions, opposite gender turned attractive, pimples started reducing & which was a little bit of redemption from my bulky list of agonies.Friends started teasing with the names we urged to be called & their chuckles proved their mischievousness.I was just getting attracted with my teen phase, suddenly i staggered a little & fell down disbalanced.The boy whom i started giving spaces on my heart, ignored me unvalued after grasping the majorest area of my heart.I became a frown, the one made only for making laughed at, concealing the pain in face with the strokes of painting brush.I understood that no phase can change my gormless life.My sixteen wasn’t that sweet .I was strived towards the locked room & crumpled bed , the only place to “ think, cry, sleep & repeat”.I stayed sheathed,with my devastated inside....

At the age of 18-

Ending of board tantrums, ending of school life,unofficial ending of some friendship & life took the turn to the passage of college life.I was a failed contender of Medical Entrance, & to my family it was that i enlisted my name in the notebook of merciless sins.I felt like forcefully presenting myself mature enough to avoid unrequited problems but unfortunately invited some extravagant spices in my life.I exaggerated that i wasn't juvenile anymore to float in the chasm of emotions & life taught me a good lesson.The more i tried to keep it simple,straightforward & uncoiled, the more it trashed me with labyrinthine wastes.Uncanny intentions of some masked people left me in utter bereavement, i was too innocent to never let them ceased coming in my life.Eyes,lips, facial expressions,gestures, humanic odours seemed irritating, started scratching my brain badly.I abused my soul for never being judgemental like others.

The hour glass noticed more shattered pieces of my life, & the flow of flooding eyes increased more...

At the age of 19-

I stopped believing on the notes of "friends forever", "BFF" & etcs.The entire world of friends, friendship & bond seems fake to me.I found every statement false which concluded with a eternal alignment of two souls. I erased the word friendship from my dictionary.I found myself vulnerable, i even hated my shadow. I wasn't able to solve the sum of life why i actually did the problems to get a handful of betrayal to be garlanded with.I arrogantly argued & searched problems in simplicity & simplicity in problems.I found my constant as the dripping tears again,this time it came as a incessant nightmare....

At the age of 21-

Break up, treachery, duplicity,health declination, dark insomniac nights, agony wrapped days, perpetual scars, indocile sternness, series of strikes, & here i find myself crawling like a living corpse.I have only seen people talking about their one inch problem as falling down in depression.& now, i have felt with my skin contaminating my whole body with its venomous syrup.I feel like embodying a lot of outrageous feelings can explode anytime smashing my organs badly.Most of the times, i find myself lying the couch of thornful thoughts, blood stained, pricked with innumerable nails & i find my soul ripped, splintered, too crispy to handle storms anymore.I feel dying in an undying pool of blaze.Now, i cry insanely so often, i don't stop until i sleep unknowingly.I remain intoxicated in my thoughts all day.The way i search my serene is writing my heart out until it fulfills my quest.I try to touch the vapours of my tear drops but they too get vanished sooner...

Broken childhood,
Unfulfilled dreams,
unending eras of pain,
continuous conversion of happiness & pain,
canvas of some unfinished pieces of stories,
flames of depression,anxiety, desolation,
duplicity in relationship,
& some more sand-made homes collapsing in a blink of eyes,

I have seen life like this way.I have felt my life have tied the knots of marriage with my unending pain.I have set a new benchmark of being the dumbest prey of depression.Neither I anymore feel ashamed with my life, nor i expect any happy rain come surprisingly to again destroy my ruined life a little more.I love death,as i have felt the gnawing peace in the silent graveyard.Endgames are always interesting, isn't it?

I wrote a new story regardless of any thoughts of its reaches.I didn't find any way better rather than being not ashamed, because nobody cares for this half dead heart, i found no way better rather than scribbling the screams that

"I AM NOT ASHAMED BEING A PREY OF ENDLESS DEJECTION, I AM NOT ASHAMED THAT I AM IN SEARCH OF EITHER RESILIENCE OR DEATH."

~©storytellersuchismita

Vandana Patel

I am Vandana Patel based in Navsari (Gujarat). I have done my degree in English literature. And I have done diploma in software development from NIIT. I write quotes, poems and articles. When I am not writing I cook and read

I love to express my thoughts through my writings. I get inspired from nature. Every natural element inspires me to think and write. Ever changing shapes of clouds or the stars in the sky make me write. The waves of the sea or calm lake both inspire me to write. When I see drops of rain or the dew , I cannot resist myself from expressing in any form of writing. I love to stare at the sky. During day clouds and at night stars invite me to have a chat with them. Another natural element what fascinates me is the sea. I get lost when I think about the depth of the sea. When I look at the waves it seems to me like thoughts of my mind. When I look at the moon, I think it observes everything silently. The moon is the only witness of my thoughts at night. And when the sun rises in the morning, it never rises alone. It rises with lots of expectations and new hope.

Here I got opportunity to write about something which we all face, but feel ashamed to express. Sooner or later we all experience these things in life. It may be stress, anxiety or depression. But no one is ready to accept. Because we think about how society will react. We are uncomfortable to talk about. People who are suffering, need help from family and friends. But they don't know how to help. We want to convey that there is nothing to be ashamed of.

How to deal with bad mood

It does not matter who you are and what you are. You are home-maker, student, businessman, sportsman, artist or anyone. Someday someway we all experience one thing. That is bad mood. Sometimes it is more than once in a day. When we get one negative comment by someone it affects our mood. Odd behavior of someone or your late schedule any of these reasons can spoil our mood. When we have bad mood we get easily irritated. We become angry on small things. All these affect our work, health, family and relationships.

Knowingly or unknowingly we suddenly feel bad. We lose interest and do not want to do anything. Just because of bad mood. Sometimes we know the reason behind it and sometimes we do not even know why we feel so bad.

Do not over think same thing again and again. Try to keep yourself busy in something else. When you think about the root cause behind your spoiled mood, it will disturb you more and things get worst. So divert your attention towards far from that reason. After sometime you may forget all that which spoiled your mood.

We all have experienced this type of feeling for so many times. Now what should be done in this situation to get out of this type of state of mind? From today whenever you feel something like this you can try one of these following ways to get back in rhythm.

1: Play With Children

Start playing with children and be like them. Forget your age, status and don't care about people around. Just get absorbed in play. Feel the innocence and honesty of children. Try to learn from them. After playing with them you will get back all your energies and excellent mood.

2: listen music:

Play some happy music and get lost in it. Music soothes your heart and soul. You will become fresh and ready to deal with anything and anyone. But never play sad songs and loud music.

3: Spend time with elders

Go to your grandparents or any elderly person in your neighborhood. Just sit with them. Talk to them or let them speak and listen to them silently. In meeting them you will learn from their experience. And they will become happy because you find time for them. In this process you will become calm and collective. Try it.

4: Meditate

Sit alone and try to relax yourself. Close your eyes and take some deep breaths. Forget everything around you. Be one with the universe. And after sometime when you will open your eyes you will feel the change in your mood and state of mind.

5: Experiment in kitchen

It is said that cooking itself is a therapy. For that you do not need to be a master chef. Anyone can cook. Just enter your kitchen and prepare anything you can. Serve your family members with love. Your efforts of cooking make you forget what is disturbing you. And you will have a new experience of cooking. It will give you satisfaction of serving food to your loved ones.

6: Go for a walk

Walking alone or with friend is a good thing. Go for a walk. Enjoy everything you see while walking. Observe small things which we generally ignore. You will take notice of those things which you have never done before. You will be surprised that how you could ignore or overlook these things. You will find that path new altogether.

7: Recollect old memories

Happy moments which we always want to cherish forever. Recollect them by watching old photo albums or anything related to your joyful experiences. Remember old school days and college days. Recall memories with friends of those days. That helps you in getting back your good mood.

8: Call someone

An old friend whom you want to talk to for days but somehow you could not. Call him/her now. This is the best time to talk to that person. After long time when you call that friend you will have a long conversation. That will relax your mood and make you remember all those happy moments which you have spent with that person. Try this it will definitely work.

My Piece Of Sky

Longing for my own sky
Give me my piece of sky
Where I could fly
Up in the sky
Without wings
In the springs
Want to see all streams
Which I have seen in dreams
No one could ask me why
There will be nothing to shy
Where I can shout so loud
My voice will be in the clouds
Stay among the stars at night
And make the world bright
Like to meet the moon
Greet and hug him soon
Craving for my own earth
Where I can make my life worth
From there I can begin all over again
My journey of happiness and gain.

Zammil

Dark velvet butterfly

Flutter, beautiful butterfly with dark velvet wings
Watching, I run towards you laughing and panting
Eyes gleam with joy for the memories it brings
But joy died suddenly and I stand addled, chanting
Wanting this fleeting emotion, as it flies away

A slight warmth tenders the heart as I think of ballet
Sometimes its faint, muddled, sometimes its strong
Gazing at the mirror I ask, when is your birthday?
These memory games are tiring, like I don't belong
Long walks along the ocean do help calm the mind

To be alive is to be grateful but it's not always kind
Words form in the mind but dissolve at the throat
Stammering and crying, this is how I am designed
But I always try to smile, to a life of alacrity I devote
Love and hope always help memories fortify

Wondering stunned at the wandering butterfly
Someone calling, rushing towards me, I turn
She grabs me hugging tight, a car speeds nearby
I can't remember her, those caring eyes I yearn
My head hurts as I cry, I remember now, "mom."

Mohita S Siddharth (Shreya)

Hi,
This is my story of 1592 words for #notashamed project.

Struggle At Every Curve

This story is about my dad and me, his name was Anurag Saran. He was the most reliable, determined and caring person in my life. He was a man who showed me different shades in life. He was born in 1956, the era when people use to stay in joint families and shared almost every thing together. He had seen the poorest to the wealthiest days in his life. Being from a family of open minded people he got all the freedom along with his 5 siblings. But he also had to face the harshest critics in his life. This story is about his struggle. He was a man of his words. Despite of his struggle he was a very jovial man. He was married at the age of 21 years to my mother Shobhana Saran. They were not happy in there life's before they were forced into marriage. My dad was working in hotel Industry so he had many dreams like he wanted to travel a lot, He wanted to be with his girl friend but when he was married he was dedicated to support mom. Although he was working very hard, 14 to 15 hours at work as he was managing a 5 star hotel as GM, He used to come home and sit with mom for hours before sleep. Then things started changing as he was getting frustrated from his life. He started to lose his temper even on small mistakes. He left his job and joined Modi group of industries. His office was in Modinagar, mom used to be a homemaker. He was become very temperamental, He used to pick up fights with mom almost every day. The day my grandparents heard about the tortures my mom was going through they spoke to my dad asked him to come and stay with them so they can take care of my mother as I was in her belly. Yes, my mom was pregnant I came into there life with my twin sister. That happiness didn't last for long my twin came into this world and we lost her because she had severe asthma and anaemia. Mom and dad were very sad, depressed. His life got to the saturation point when I started fainting every now and then in school starting from nursery class. He was very much in shock to know my heart is too weak, I suffer from genetic disorder I am also severely anaemic and he started being extra conscious with me. He used to work really hard to fulfil all our needs. But he used to be angry at times and it was very disturbing to see that he struggled to express his emotions. He used to raise his hand on mom. She used to get hurt, wounded but she never complaint to anyone. Years passed and one day when it was my 17th birthday something bad happened and I was not able to shake off the feeling of not being trusted by my father. As I was very close to my dad, I told him i am going to college early morning and would come home by 8:30pm or 9pm. He said okay go and enjoy yourself. I got a strange call from my mom at 8pm "why I am not at home your grandmother is brain washing your dad and he is very angry". I told her I am coming home would reach in 20 minutes and hung up the phone. When I reached home without even saying a word my dad slapped me for the first time in 17 years. I was in shock, I started crying and ran to my room, I didn't knew how to react or express my anger, so I just locked my room and broke everything I had decorated my room with, and slept without eating food. That was the worst birthday of my life. Next day, I woke up at 6am got ready and left for college and told mom I won't be coming home from hostel for dad, and they don't need to bother about my needs I have got a job I will pay for my studies and fulfil my daily needs. Mom was depressed I told my brother to take care of mom and if dad ever tries to raise his hand on mom call me i will deal with him. I left with tears in my eyes. Months passed my professor and friends at college forced me to go home for my birthday again but I refused and as dad was missing me he called said "What have I done that broke your heart? Let's just meet once like old times go for a movie and talk out our difference". I asked him why did you slap me in front of all the people you called to celebrate my birthday? He said I am very sorry, your grandmother came that day and said you are having an affair and you roam Around with this guy named Anand, and she doesn't like him and his family. I told me I have a boyfriend and you have met him yes he is Anand and I go out with him but not without telling you. I have never hidden any of my secrets from you then why did I get that punishment. You could have told grandmother that you knew what I was doing in my personal life was not her concern. What's the point in telling the truth and getting slapped when I am doing nothing wrong. I asked dad what is going on why there was a change of heart for me? He said he was told that I am a rebel, I don't care what freedom means? He was shocked, hurt and frustrated and this exaggerated situation led to slapping me. Although he apologised several times I was not convinced and told him i would never come back home and don't want to talk to him or see him. He went home and didn't talk to anyone for 2 years. Finally, my college result was out and he called to congratulate me as I became a doctor. I started my internship in City hospital, pusa road when one day my day called and said I want you to come home in evening have to talk something very important. At first I denied but then i said if I get free early I would definitely come. When I reached home mom my brother were very happy and everyone pampered me. But i could feel my dad was not fine, He seemed weak, malnutrition and depressed. I walked up to him and he said I want eat something made by you so I made his favourite dish and fed him with my hands. First bite he started weeping and said I am sorry for what I did, I can't stay happy if my diamond is not shining bright, I said I forgave you long ago please don't be sad and stop crying, tell me what is wrong with you are you alright. He said I won't survive this for more than a month. You stay happy. I was shocked to hear this and I panicked, I called my grandparents to ask what has been going on with dad and why is he not well? They started blaming me. I disconnected there call and started looking for reports, it felt like the earth beneath my feet was moved dad was suffering from bone fever also known as meningitis and he was also severely anaemic, He was in fever for last 1 year and never went to doctor. I called my younger brother who was staying in Lucknow asked him to come back to Delhi as dad needs us now. Next morning i took him for proper check up and we came to know that he was at the last stage and would not survive for more a 3 weeks. He collapsed on the way to city hospital and I was blank. I called my collegues at work to get dad admitted and in few days my dad passed away. His last words in his consciousness were to the other doctors " Don't touch me, only my daughter would treat me , She is my diamond and she would shine bright" and he went unconsious for ever. I stayed in hospital all the time I knew every moment I was losing him I went into severe depression, I became violent the day he left us. I was guilty of not talking to him for 2 years. But it was not my fault that he felt ill. It took me one year to prove myself innocent after my family abandoned me the day my day was cremated, my family told everyone that I died the day my dad died,this destroyed my medical career, I was hopeless, I had not will to live. But my friends helped me overcome my pain and I am #notashamed for being stubborn, not guilty any more as I was not the reason for my dad's death and I proudly say that I am my dad's daughter, still following my dad's footsteps. He taught me to be independent at a very young age, fight for what is right, learn from my mistakes and never turn your back on family and stay strong just like a mountain so no storm can tear you apart. I love you dad..

" Success comes at a price, that price is not bigger than your family"

- Mohita S Siddharth (Shreya)

Aashna Aga

Myself, Miss. Aashna Aga, belongs to Goa - A girl with "Honey Heart", flowing imagination and words in her veins...

Love to inhale Incredible words , and try to put them into Imagical verses..My biggest inspiration is my Mom.

I have a craze for Poetry since long but,talent remain hidden. And now situation made me to increase my passion towards writing. And today I am "An Incredible Queen of My Poetic Kingdom" and waiting for that day when I will have a tag of "Poetess" .

Mirakee pen name :
©queen_of_words_ashu

Insta ID:
Mywords_mygem2204

GRAPPLING WITH MENTAL DILEMMA

Taunt of world as I won't succeed,
Listening all these my eyes bleed,
Their disgusting words letting me down,
Making my face grow frown,
Scars given by others I am not hiding,
And the way towards success I am still finding,
My memory is bit low,
Still good thoughts my imagination blow,
I am not mentally stable, I am weak,
Yet my flaws I gracefully try to kick,
I do mistake, but still I try,
And not letting others to know my inner cry,
No one is Understanding my inner voice and neither feel it,
Awarded me reason to stop my heart beat,
Made me suffer from pain,I was ditched by life,
I was dying for smile, everywhere I found strifes,
Although to tell these Someone will feel ashamed,
But, yeah, telling you frankly, I am not ashamed...
©queen_of_words_ashu

THE MOMENT: RINGED BY ABASEMENT

Not a girl, but the guy was her best friend,
Once walking on the road, just she had hold his hand,
Soon, rumors begins to spread very quick,
Which let her grew mentally weak
The torture by family gifted her pain,
She turned mad, thinking about this again and again,
The fever of depression was getting high,
The evil of loneliness was not ready to say goodbye,
Head suppressed under the ocean of depression,
Mind preparing to face the world's deadly questions,
Negative comments distracting her from direction,
Letting life to lose it's peace and satisfaction,
Everywhere there was rejection,
Drowning in the canyon of tension,
But, she gave herself a space,
Talked with her own self to find proper ways,
That talk with herself gave her fortitude,
To face all these, she strongly stood with attitude,
And the narrow mind thinking of people she blamed,
And yes, to share all these she did not feel ashamed...
©queen_of_words_ashu

DEPRESSION: POISONOUS GIFT BY SOCIETY

"She, she can't do anything" this what they said,
This one statement let her to be sad,
Whenever she was about to face Something with positivity,
She felt as if tied up with the pillar of negativity,
Neglected by family, dejected by everyone,
All these let her smile to burn,
Pretending to be ok when actually she was not,
With her mental dilemma she strongly fought,
Dark clouds of loneliness busted over her,
Letting her happiness path to be blur,
But she, swipe away every gloominess,
And made a space for breeze of freshness,
Just because she was lonely,
Just because she was only,
To face the difficulties of life, she was not ashamed,
To do face off with pain, she was not ashamed...
©queen_of_words_ashu

"NO MORE RELUCTANT"

The deep scars over my soul I don't want to hide,
I am not ashamed to confess "That failure is by my side,
I am not ashamed to say "I have lost my originality",
I am not ashamed to say "I am facing worst reality",
I am not ashamed to say "I am failure",
I am not ashamed to say "My pain is uncured",
I am not ashamed to say "I am surrounded by violence",
I am not ashamed to say "I have lost my solace",
I am not ashamed to say "I am feeling insecure",
I am not ashamed to say "My dreams are no more pure",

In depression net when you are caught,
You will be just bound by negative thoughts,
But, you don't pretend to be someone which you are not...

The dust of anxiety you try to wipe,
All your stress and fear you try to swipe...

If you will be ashamed today,
You have to face all these everyday,
So,stay physically fit not mentally ill,
By defeating weakness , your anxiety you kill.....
©queen_of_words_ashu

STOP MOLESTING....
START PROTECTING

Just because "she" is a girl,
Is she required to cross ocean of trouble??
When she doesn't bleed at her first night, is she no more virgin?
If she wears short dress, jeans and t-shirts, is she characterless?
If she hold friendship with boys, is she shameless?

Build the thoughts of humanity within you,
Try to look a lady with good view,
Rather than staring at her Divine beauty,
To appreaciate and support is your duty,
Inspire her to be strong in her life,
Rather than encircling her with grief and strife,
Show your altruism, be a gentleman,
Put a fire and burn your inner demon...

Neither I am not ashamed to fight for rape extinction,
Nor I am ashamed to do this discussion,
Some might be feeling shame to share all this,
But I am not ashamed any more to clarify all this,
Your narrow mind thinking you try to beat,
Either make it broader or just change it....
©queen_of_words_ashu

Sujindran. B

Sujindran. B, Suchindrum, Kanyakumari, 629704.

A man being born in a divine landmark, on getting, writing as the only skill set, from my engineering graduation, and compassion as the one from my living, I began my way through this existence, as having Civil services as the primary goal. They say a lot of history, a lot and lot of peculiarly man-made conflicts and consequences, where the one thing that allured me were the changes. How come after all this calamity, change prevailed so far, with only changing its theme over times. Living may seem like, it's all about how broad we shine. But life's something like, survival of our own. And when I got my very first opportunity from KALON MAPLE PUBLISHING, indeed, that's the moment where I felt true, everyone's given a life only for living and how the one lives, is entirely up to them. As no one ever said before, 'Every ones story, has its own glory'.

So, at the keyboard I could see, as for the sake of human advancement and communication, there are 26 keys of alphabets. Yet, when I try to put out something that's thriving in my awareness, I couldn't see abundant blend of possible phrases to describe them all. Though I couldn't even express them all, so as to describe it. Waiting for the conclusion of my 23 years of impelling existence, I've still not perceived, whether is there an issue with myself or the world I'm existing in. It drains me out, knowing something's odd around myself, not remarking what the fact really is. It's an utter irony to say, many days of life has been just gone, in attempts of figuring out those. I'm still on the count so far in the quest, which seems a bizarre fantasy to many eyes and souls. The expedition to see myself, living with desire and happiness. Not only over the things that I seek, but also those came seeking me. There glimmered one pair of eyes, the one that I never got tired on looking in for hours, days and nights. I saw the whole world within, or to say, my whole world within those gorgeous eyes. That maybe something a little more to get obsessed with, but the list goes on to reach out the stars, when those days just went through all of my living, flooding my soul and conscience with so much ecstasy to desire the will to nothing but to live. Particularly there, the moments of living never longed much effort from my side, for their nourishment. But I got to feel the essence of life, only after perceiving those eyes. So, the soul of those eyes was not something I desired in this impelling existence, but something that made me, to live the life I'm living, with desire. It certainly drove me to a mile where I went utterly whelmed, when life too, taught me an inspiring fact of nothing but falling. And the scene sequenced well with nothing but losing. Well, the things that I've lost, were not ought to leave with the memories behind, but after all, they did. It's just that I thought my life and this person were just one after all, but only a little later that I unproven, I am wrong once again, when that one drifted off the path apart from the one that I'm walking. I'm not sure of a proper way to talk with this life, so I'll try to put up with words, yet I lack most the places due to my own immaturity. Still I loathe the actions that are made bluntly under the labels of maturity. Days mostly ended up with nights where I'm throwing out questions on what's and how's and some little why's. And nights often wrapped up with days blooming with much opportunities, for seeking and solving the last night mysteries. Life is an utter oblivion sometimes, yet it drives to be a mystical intimacy at some points. To say frankly, just one or some sequence of chapters aren't enough to decide the wild nature, this life holds. Yet to know and feel certain facts and measures, one person is all it takes to teach me all, apart from the preaching of life as well as myself. One person, it takes for me to, grasp the whole constellation within my hold, and just the same one, for me the loathe the whole existence that I'm living, right now. The way that I feel towards life, is same as that I feel towards my parents and also it felt the same as for that one person of mine, but only in such rewinding. The vivacity of breathing will occur only when one's aware of the reality, the one's living. In pursuit of writing, a writer will eventually reach a point where he'll be overwhelmed with the voices so as to end up with no words of choice, or a point where he'll be just holding the pen, over a blank page so as to end up with no voices or anything at all. Life may not give things that I wish for, or crave for, not all the times. But it does throws out some handouts and plays, that will surely leave me stumbled or stunned to the heaven and hell. What I'm seeing might be linked with, what I might have wished to see, not all the times. But I never got the custom as dropping, the desire to wish. What I speak, mostly does sync with, what's that went on my mind, not all the times. Since much many were just smothered and faded away, at the very point where they appeared. While getting older with time, life just kept on bringing such dares, where I would just blunder as much as get lost, on attempts to get over, or right through them. Mostly, I would just sit over the point where I faltered, just a little puzzled on what to do after all. The act, that I got up, doesn't mean that the mystery's been cracked, but sitting around doing nothing pains more than the trips, I got. And by the times when I've been eventful with my head, the heart blunted most of its skills, at least for my sake, it kept on pumping. From the stories and tales that I professed so far, I don't think of much aspects, as measured to be a shame, for a human individual. In fact, as for myself, waning to live the existence that I'm provided with, is the only shame, that I would ever remorse. Though being born as a human among enormous diversities of wild nature, is something that dawdles amongst a profanity and a boon. So, the authenticity of life is something inimitable for each and every living, just something not to be fairly underrated or hyped, just because we got to clutch it. This life will never bounce me a hint on, what'll be certain to myself or, what'll be snatched away from myself, at a distance from the wishes and outlooks, I had. That's it, be mindful of what you do, even when you do nothing.

Aarthi Sampath

I am Aarthi Sampath, Artist based in Chennai, 37 yr old, I have muscular Dystrophy and I use wheelchair,Pet lover,Painting was my profession,

But now I am a writer, I have written lots of articles about me, and I write to break stigma, and against bullies, I love to write about,self-love,.self-aware

I'm a co author of Anthologies "clipped wings grow", "Letters to self","Untold, Unwritten Unheard", Hashtag "#metoo"

"clipped wings glow"

which has been published, and some more upcoming anthologies too.

I am Thankful for Kalon Maple Publishing

And Mrunaal Gawhande And Komal

For these excellent Anthologies and for Encouraging Writers Like me. And I Glad to join this team Yet Another celebration hashtag #not_ashamed

To show concern for mental health issues,To stand in solidarity with everyone else to End this Stigma, and

Not to be Ashamed of any medical condition,Cause we own our body, mind and soul.

My motto

"Write what you witness that "witnessed your existence"

My instagram id aarthisampath_

This is about someone else who once told about their condition,
And the words are purely mine.

I survived

I lay awake as
the fog settles in my mind
and I'm finding my voice,
Drowning when I tried to scream;
I'm tangled in fire and ice,
as my demons Ripped me;
I couldn't move as the numbness
creeped in me,
I can hear my loved ones calling my name but I feel my vocal muted;
I feel like drowning into an avalanche, Sending Chills down my spine
I hear my heart pounding and I became
Inconspicuous to myself,
I scream to let me free,
Some people call me clumsy
they don't know the demons screaming in me, and ruling my mind,
the demons Yelling me to free them, To slash my wrist, to strangle myself
They say I am unhappy and laugh at me,
The demons make me hate myself
that I am ugly, some days they will pretend to be my friends talking in my mind,
they say people hate me and trying to kill me,
Somedays I feel like world is ending,
On other days I am overwhelming with happiness and that days my pills
Shush my demons to stay away;

I want this to end and to be bold,
I wanted to end this stigma,
I am trying to help myself that I wanna
ignore the demons in me, I am trying to rise before my demons eat me,
I am trying to be me, to feel my worth
before I get drowned;
I am finding my voice to speak up,
I want to survive and not ashamed
To ask for help
I don't wanna a give up as I am
Not Ashamed to tell this world
I survived.

* * *

This is about someone who suffer with tourette syndrome and It's called tics, schizophrenia and some associated disorders.

Unpredictable

She became unpredictable
Fighting a battle everyday
Echoes in her head are never ending,
Pulsating her heart with panic attacks
Tightened her chest that she gasp for breath;
She became unbearable
Swinging moods rock her, with
bouts of crying for no reason;
She sometimes looks at the ceiling
For long periods as her demons in her,
Mind is the dictator of her world;

She became unacceptable
As her mind goes blank for long periods
she Constantly Blinks her eyes for no reasons,
sometimes her voice make peculiar sounds, and she constantly shrugs her
Shoulders unaware of herself;
Sometimes she hallucinate as demons in her mind Are driving her crazy,
And they're blocking her loved one's attempts to save her;
the demons Speak to her,
making her respond to every question arise, they frighten her by telling
Her that she might be labelled
The demons pushing her to the edge of nowhere, But she's Not
Ashamed to open up to pour her heart out,
To seek help;
She became unknown entity to herself,
and Pills make her calm and giddy,
Made her lethargic and undesirable,
Yet she's Not Ashamed to tell this world,
That Sometimes God too must be crazy.

Setha Soni

Setha Soni is an aspiring CA. from Bhubaneswar Odisha. New to the world of writing and loving the experience yet.

#1.miss_the_old_me

I am messed up inside out., when they ask, I lie
my lips say, fine, thank you.
but my eyes tell a different story,
my heart sings a different tune,
and my soul just weeps,
cause my mood doesn't just swing,
it bounces, pivot, rebound and fluctuates,
it is all that happens in a blink.
people think its sadness, it's crying
it is depression dressing me in blind
but how wrong they are ., replacing numb with some.
it's being numb to emotion ., it's being numb to life
I wake up in the morning just to go back to bed again in some while
in all this chaos,
I felt so scared and so alone, the coldness fills my every bone
sleep isn't sleeping anymore, it been an escape since long
I miss the old me, the happy me, the gone me.
I am messed up inside out when they ask, I say
I am depressed, but not giving up.

#2.solitary_zone

surrounded by people, yet all alone,
trapped within his solitary zone
a world where chaos and hate overtake,
every bit of happiness that may try to escape
laughter and smiles never seem to last
because I am haunted by memories of my past
running the distance with nowhere to go
these are the days of my life a Broadway show
where emptiness weighed the most.
I wanted to speak, scream and shout but all I could was a whisper,'i am fine now'.
cause I can never expose you, never tell the truth about you, about your existence
you are my punisher, my captor and my torturer,
you are the little voice echoing in my head tormenting me all day long
breaking the women who was once very strong.
each day is like reliving a bleak dream, every 24 hrs. repeating exactly the same
when the tension becomes too great I'm forced to distract myself with a different form of pain.
moon and stars do not provide enough light for this darkness in my mind
and hope drains my soul, as, hope is an illusion an optimist's prediction.
I have had enough now.i'm not you, never was and never will be
I'm above this, above you, above it all, and I will survive
life in recovery may not be the same, rules may have changed in this brand new game
you can pick up the pieces and make a new start
and your courage and hope will keep you away from falling

apart
surrounded by people yet all alone,
trapped within his solitary zone

Muskan Gupta

Muskan gupta, is 18-year old and is currently pursuing her engineering in computer science. She started writing for about one year ago. For her, Writing is not only her hobby but also it's a perfect balm to all the bruises she comes across in life and it's the only way she describes her feelings and emotions. She writes about pain, also romantic pieces to raising voice against every social evil through her writings. She generally writes non-fiction, so the same she contributed writing in this book. Inked moments, is her first book she has contributed in.

She expresses herself in form of long poems and write-ups. When and wherever anything stucks her mind she starts to scribble down her emotions. As being introvert by nature, pen and paper are her best friends. She speaks less and let her words communicate. Besides, Writing she is interested in music, the very other way she relates herself and finds peace in. As important is writing, so is reading to her. She reads a thousands books and let her words flow like a river. She pours down everything in mind, to let go her sorrows and to reborn courage in her.

"Life is beautiful just as bed of roses but it has challenges too which are like thorns".

The journey of being a bud to blossom into a flower is full of struggles. Sometimes, it blown away by wind. Sometimes it plucks down due to rain. After all it struggles, it shows it's true colours. Similarly is the life of people, we go through blossoming process. Yes the process is always not the same..but it's end is though the same.. Something beautiful!! My journey of survival began 18 years back.

The first most fun-filled part of anyone's life" The childhood". When I as a bud started to open up my petals to this world. I was also blessed with childhood like any another happy go lucky child. But this innocence and childhood peace was scratched and sucked up by the demons of social evil "CHILD ABUSE". I am a child abuse survivor. A child who was physically abused but I am not ashamed to accept it. Though it was not that painful as a child because it was too hard to understand of what was actually happening? Whether it was right or wrong..? There was always a feeling of something bad happening but confidence over took that feeling. So as a small child I did whatever I was told to do. The touch overall gave a very uncomfortable feeling. It is painful to come face to face with the reality that you were abused as a child. It is even painful and depressing to acknowledge that another human could have treated you that way, especially when you encounter that another person was someone you loved, in my case he was my so called cousin brother on whom not only you as a child believed with eyes closed but also parents. How hurtful and frightening it was to feel that way that way as child of five year. It wasn't a long term abuse. But abuse is abuse. A five year old child did not deserve what she struggled.

Taking a leap to now long 5 years more when you start to know about society. During this leap of five years when my parents constantly put me to training...that what to do if u come across something like this, or someone like this...especially the most important part of my life was me being fat. I was a bubbly child which everyone admired and wanted to play with as being when they are child but when they become bit old being fat they are socially unacceptable and always pin pointed as being "out of the box". My mind struggled understanding this. Then after there was throbbing in the head relating this. A period when my mind could experience pain much more than my body. There was a feeling of guilt, a feeling of shame as a child. There was always constant unusual fear which I carried heavy in my heart. A fear at the bus stop in going to school to a fear of facing any male in the society. And that distancing from people started. I became much mature than my age. I turned to an introvert who finds their own company the best. There I was able to sense family issues and struggles so thinking wisely and maturely I never felt like discussing it with my parent. Rather alone I was facing and overcoming this. I became expert in hiding my feelings in order to protect myself from the torrent of the abuse. It was easier to deny your feelings rather than facing criticism and rejection. This reaction was an automatic response which probably goes on, even though when I am an adult now. Dealing with constant trust issues, carrying heavy load of buried emotions from the past. It ruined my teenage as well terribly leading to all insecurities. Teenager ,a transition stage. It is a tenure when you become responsible for all your actions. You change emotionally, physically, socially, mentally and in every way one can.

As I described above I was a bubbly child which when turns into a fat teen is not accepted by society. You are being unnecessarily given advices and even illogical solutions which hearing whole day long makes you feel frustrated and unwanted and also you start to question why me? Proportionally, thousands of things was going in mind. It was a tenure when i struggled to recognize my identity. So whole of the teenager I was struggling as a teenager trying to fit in a societal condones. It created obstruction in pursuing things which I liked or admired doing. There were thousands of things for which my eyes used to fill with tears.... But overall I got a feeling that it is unwise to count on others for my needs and emotional dealing but to count only upon myself. And I got used to all the pains, and life came to normalcy, I drank to drown all my pain, but the dammed pain learned how to swim. As a grown up teenager of almost of 15 years old, Depression suddenly hits me. I felt like there is light at the end of the tunnel which is about to blow anytime. At the same I felt pain which would probably never end. I knew I was not normal, something was happening to me, something which could not be described. Something which was just taking a lot of my energy... there was no excitement in living life, I felt lifeless, there was peace in rest. At the same time so much restlessness waking up and pushing up myself to school was a big struggle. Where I saw other children enjoying school days. I was dragging myself to school. That hundred percent attendee was now escaping from school. Every morning I used to come up with an excuse to my parents for escaping from school, parents also did not encounter it as a serious issue, and was probably regarded as any other teenager drama. Fear of being judged, I never shared this with anyone and fought this battle alone and all being alone facing it. I used to break down often.

I got conscious of facing people as something worrying always visible on my face whatever was going in my mind. The feeling was exhausting. It was suffocating ..There was pity and discomfort and also there was emptiness in my stomach. I felt alone even when I was surrounded by the whole crowd. Everything was dark. There was no sunshine in head. I was turning into absolute pessimist. I also lost my apetite... like I took a lot of time in eating than my normal routine because I used to get lost while eating in some other world... When i used to get ready for school I took too much time than normally I took... Parents noticed this as titled as laziness. And when I use to go school. I used to sit in some corner alone, away from everyone. I turned into an emotionless creature from caring girl I turned into careless girl. Neither there were tears seeing others in pain nor there was happiness in others happiness. So it was overall a 2- 3 months long deression tenure which drived away all my happiness, all my energy, all my hope. But it had to end. The first step is always the hardest from usually watching suicide videos to thinking over committing suicide. I began to watch motivation , counting my blessings , a major help and counsellor was my mother. I started connecting to her. we had long talks and discussed things and then finally healing through spirituality. Faith and hope which never died in me. And it took me out from this period also.

Mental pain or illness is hard to reveal.It is easier to say my "tooth is broken than to say that my heart is aching or heart is broken". But the first time always has to be there, which takes a lot of guts and strength. But staying silent is also not a choice because Staying silent means staying isolated.Staying isolated means staying sick.Staying sick means staying worried. Staying worried means to staying ashamed....

And This is my story and I AM NOT ASHAMED.

Veena Sharma

Name : veena sharma

Poetical Name : Shashiinderjeet

Profession : Lecturer in English

Hobbies : Reading and writing literature in Hindi, urdu and english

Special interest : Painting, photography and fashion designing

Acknowledgement : Best Teacher Award

Publications : Co auther in 8 Anthologies

Ishq-e-watan (Hindi)
Clipped Wings Grow. (English)
Letters to Self. (English)
Ala Rasi. (Hind)
#Me Too. (English)
anthology for Fall. (English)

Clipped Wings glow (English)

Life Regained

The struggle that knocked the innocent heart
With a strong blow to hurt fully my heart
Unbelievable and unbearable was this jerk
This shock overpowered my veins of heart
Depression made my life a hell
Scared of every ringing bell
Closed all the doors of my mind
Only the roaring pains roped me to bind
A wrestle of negative thoughts was there
To throw me down in the ring of depression
It thrashed me badly , I twisted
Floundering badly , I was in full depression
Now I lost my thoughts
No wishes , no efforts , no worries , no problems to me
Each and everything became meaningless to me
Not ahsmed that being egoist ,I rose myself to that point
Where my life filled with a hundred of challenges
Getting thrashes again and again by the luck I lost my balances
I was cursed and abused but my parents were with me
My sibblings also positively handled me
The efforts brought fruit and they filled a confidence in me
Love and sympathy played a great role
And I was again in the nice stage of the world to play a big role

Dumb Senses

My heart is in a deep shock
My heart is now in intensive care unit
critically injured by the stonepelters of emotions
That stuck badly to shatter me as a whole
As helpless fellow looking for love and sympathy
No body was there to follow my pathy
I was deaf and dumb at all
My senses were going weak at all
The feelings of my heart were imprisoned in mind
My mind changed the thoughts
Initiated to mobile the thoughts
Tried to create a new piece of heart as an art
My heart beat was coming normal and now my body was hot
Life welcomed me again and my beats were at love shot
I thanked the God who blessed me
Brought me again in the world that was snatched from me

Isolation

A cobweb of isolation created a thick net
And trapped me very badly
Wriggling in the cobweb , I was a butterfly
Fluttering my little thin wings badly
I was helpless , it was impossible to come out
Of this critical situation
Hopes were dying , nothing was there , except
The derisive laughing of the devil of isolation
Squirming in this unbearable condition
I began to cry high and high but the cruel isolation
Could n't dare to sympathise me in painful condition
Now   it was the time a ray of love and sympathy
That peeped through the window of my mind
And I felt some spiritual stregth in my mind
The mind immidiatly communicated every cell
To pull my body from this hell
And a fluke welcomed me the next moment
I was set free in the next moment
I flew and entered in my heaven
Thanked my God to regain me, my heaven
I'm not ashamed that I fell in a shell due to my own weakness
But feel good playing in the lap of positiveness

Dr. Meghana Sree Ravali Puranapanda

Mirakee I'd : dr_meghana_sreeravali
Instagram I'd : meghanapuranapanda
Mail I'd : meghana.puranapanda@gmail.com

Namasthe..!!

Myself Dr.Puranapanda Meghana Sree Ravali as only daughter of world's best parents ..Puranapanda Sri Krishna and Maha Lakshmi , I feel so proud.Their love and support is the only radiant path that engulfed my darkest hours and moulded me into a simple being knowing the worth of a life and acts of karma.I'm a Dentist graduated recently,citizen of India,native of Kakinada, Andhra Pradesh.

I'm a passionate singer of Carnatic Music and a Diploma holder of Music.I'm an artist who tries to depict the magical romance of nature and portraits pure bonds through my pencil illustrations.Oscillating in words of cloaked dreams I started weaving my bleeding thoughts onto paper as scribbler from long but voice of my inner struggle carved and reached out for the wide platform because of writer's community in Mirakean world and I sincerely thank KalonMaple Publishing House for paving a spectacular path of Anthologies in which I'm happy to be a part in this Special Anthology of Mental Health Awarness - Not Ashamed.Apart from Anthologies - Shades of Frozen Fear and Audacity of Blank Page this is my 3rd Anthology as a co-author.

Never Be Ashamed

Stop pretending okay when actually not
As greatest trouble is with own intellect thought

Break inner stigma of silent rains
Usher mental illness knot's gaze
Uncover hidden scars and pains
Reveal trapped sorrowful maze

Never be ashamed to stage real you
By holding faulty genetics and traumatized past
Create a change that last and true
For rendering shades of lively mast

Snap out of bias
Smash the silence
And Accept the colored mark

Forgotten Memories..Dementia..

Encased in closed wall
Left afar is myself awol
Lost track of live life
As captive in past rife

Horror flick of darkened day
Sorrow encrust present stay
Visual hallucination to out-focus
Memories omit memories

Saddened behind verse
Confused beyond concept
Do not scold,cry or curse
I can't help the way I enact

To love and stand by me
And lend warmth in bend
As patience accompany thee
Is all that I ask till end

As Depressed Mind it is..!
The Villian of Dementia..!!

Hurried Thoughts Of Anxiety

Enslaved in cloaked vault of fears
Presuming every possible bruise
With mystic panic spheres
Gliding on uneasiness cruise

In battle of if's to horizon of chills
With sweaty body and tensed stare
Oversensitive to emotional spells
As exaggerated thoughts pair

Trapped in own uncaged wrath
Of palpitations, insomnia and freak outs
I create myself a tough life path
By stressing on all point routes

Caress me for pain and joy
Love me with unconditional norms
In addition to psychotherapic ray
To unbind my twitchy storms

Yes..I think everything so deep..!
And end up as an anxious steep..!!

Rishika Jakhar

Hi, my name is Rishika Jakhar. I am 19 years old.I am from Chandigarh. Currently I am pursuing engineering from PEC University of Technology. I am a second year student in Materials and Metallurgical engineering. I started writing at the age of 16 on the mirakee app. I enjoy reading novels and poetry. My favorite poets are Walt Whitman and Slyvia Plath. Apart from that, I describe myself best as as " a walking contradiction".

#not_ashamed

Leave me as it is
I like being lonely,
Why should I explain my love for melancholy?
It's my escape from uncertainty of emotions
This sadness is all I have
I can't let go of it
All these hues of dusk within me,
My mottled light will resurrect a thousand moons.
- Rishika Jakhar

#not_ashamed

My words have failed to describe
The state of my helplessness
So I wish my silence had a voice
So you all could hear
The howling of my soul
The weeping of my heart
As I take a leap into the black hole of my past
To meet myself again.

In an attempt
To express the ineffable pain
That has anguished me to silence,
I write.
To get closer to a fiction I wished was a reality,
I write.
To contribute my verse to the songs of the cosmos,
I write.
To love someone I know wouldn't love me back,
I write.
I write, to rise from the ashes and fall in the heavens.
- Rishika Jakhar

Palak Jaggi

Palak Jaggi is a high school graduate,college student and a budding writer. Her day to day life is the inspiration behind her works.Her way with words is what attracts the readers.Her motive is to produce such narratives and poetries which people can relate to.In her leisure time she likes to write, paint and read books.She believes that writing and painting are some of the ways through which people can express their feelings.Playing with words and bringing out deep and inspiring meaning and conveying it to people is what she's working on.

Not ashamed

Not ashamed for being blamed
For the mistakes that I made
These mistakes provide me shade
By the experience that I have gained.

Not ashamed for the less that I talk
For my little words don't create a mess in someone's life's walk.

Not ashamed for the nature that I possess
For it helps many to lose their stress.

Not ashamed for the path that I choose
Even if I get confuse
I'll try once more for the passion that I boost
As I refuse to lose.

Malavika Vipin

Malavika Vipin is an insightful Indian writer, native of God's own country,Kerala. Co-author of the anthology 'Audacity of the blank pages: Writerstolli'. She is an enthusiastic Virgoian with many talents. Rashtrapati Guide(Bharat Scouts and Guide). Her mission is to empower the world with education to build humanity and love.

Inspired by her parents Thekkedath Vipin and Bindu Vipin, understanding their social responsibility started Indobiocoal industries,Kerala to tackle the problems in fuel sector with biomass energy production. Blessed with a sister Mrudula Vipin, her motivator.Being an empathetic person, which help her lot in writing.

Connect through malavikavipin123@gmail.com
https://hellopoetry.com/u727093/
http://www.mirakee.com/malavikavipin

Awfully quiet

Scribbled words of the shattered soul
Often missed the rhythm
Beckons the Beamish world
Upon her, with the lost trust
Intractable pain horned
Tremendous grief...
Crawls on the ocean
Breath away! Away from the noises
Into the blockade of silence
She became awfully quiet!

The flavour of arrogance spread her world
The distraction and hatred garnish her life
What else, the atrocities and violence whirled
And it sprouts the fear and distress in life
Ultimate chaos emancipates her as a psycho.

Not ashamed! These pains and fears
Will become her strength one day.

Thunder

Thunder strike into my future
It burns everything
Ashes of hope and dream
Flattered in the air.

A deep void in the heart
Create extreme vulnerabilities in the mind
And the debris of past whirls up
Like the gusty wind of pressurised belt

In the night deep fear hooks up
As if a thunder monsters
With his silver skeletal body
And delicate silver sharp nails
Scratch my whole life again and again
Sense deep pain in the soul.

Life craves for the relief
But the prison of storms
Become thicker and thicker
Tramples me forever...

I will fight back, as a warrior
Not ashamed anymore, brave enough!

Not ashamed

A jumble of thought strikes suddenly
I'm confused
These disorganised thoughts become my lifelong struggle
Delusions! The door with seven locks, the twisted candles
With feathers, the valley of ghosts...
These noises, is it a mere hallucination of mine?
Masquerading all these into one
And they claimed I had got 'dementia praecox'
Exactly the 'Schizophrenia'!
Erratic, I'm not sick
I can see more, hear more, analyse more
Not ashamed, I'm blessed with the super powers
You don't understand
You don't want to trust

Aryan Arun

Once upon a time... I asked for something, from The Almighty God. I asked Him to free me, Free me from this Agony, This pain that resides inside me. It wasn't until later, When I realized that God... He doesn't work like that, No Sir.

So... I took a Hammer. Laid it down on those two Culpable Souls, Found harassing a little Innocent Boy. When I was done... Putting them to the ground. The Agony, A part of my persona, until then... Was gone. For the moment, at least. Was it because of God, I asked?

A Wise Man had once said... He doesn't work that ways.

So, I took the law into my own hands... To take out my pain on those who are guilty for it. When it was all done for... I asked for forgiveness. I'm still waiting for Him... To shed a light on my Repentant Mortality.

Fancy start, isn’t it? A fairy tale would've suited better. That's how my life was... At least for a while, At least in the beginning. It wasn't perfect but It was damn close. A dysfunctional yet loving family, consisting of a Archangel, though Clean freak of one half of the parents and a not so great... Demonic Perdition of a father.

And Me... What about me? Just a broken soul... Couldn’t bear to be repackaged. My well being, everyday, was hanging through a thin thread. Waiting one day... It'll fall in Insanity. Why all this negativity? My life... Personally... My history?

Molested at a tender age... Then again and then again. Three times, A secret I share with my insides. Never had the guts to tell anyone. Maybe I should have... Would have saved this feeling of having a ball of guilt and anger and shame inside me.

The Mental harassment from mentors and one half of the aforementioned parent. The fear of not being good enough. Everything was wrong.

Yet, I made do with it. I always did... Somehow, Someway. My mind couldn't bear to even think of letting down the people who I cared so much about, Family, that is.

With a new life around the horizon... Comprising of a New School, New Courses, New Subjects and of course, New people. People... What I wouldn't give to have a connection with them. Everywhere I looked... People. Connecting, Socializing, Enjoying, Having the time of their life. Then there was me... The Outlaw. The outcast who liked being alone. If only they knew that how hard it was... For someone like me to connect with them. They didn't understand and I thought they never will, No one will, as a matter of fact.

Suddenly, One fine day... The fearful hand of loneliness took control of my once Innocent and Delighted soul. Earlier, where it was joy... Now there was agony. Where there was Compassion... Now there was Vexation. Before I knew it.. My mind was falling into the Abyss of what the society called Depression.

I thought I could deal with it... It was just my mind playing games with me, Nothing new. I've been dealing with stuff like this my whole life, I'll get through. Only this time... I couldn't. My mind was weak, My Moral was weak, I... was weak. I felt like I'd let everyone down and I did.

What started as A new life, Though not wanted but still useful, had started to, now, come crashing down. School was done for as My mind couldn't fathom the pressure, anymore. Home was ripped apart with the loss of an already distant parent... Seemed like My life was already done for. My depression had gotten the better of me.

As days went by, I started losing the track of my emotions... My feelings... They all went away. I had become hollow inside. A hollow human being... Or was I? Could I have still considered myself a human? I had no attributes needed to be one. I was the outcast... An Alien. An Alien who doesn't know how or what to feel. So, I started observing. Observing the people around me. Their behavior, their emotions... I wished that I one day... I could get them back.

For the time being, I had learnt to pretend. The subtle art of pretense where I was faking all my human emotions. I know how a lot of people, like me, they fake conversations, too. I, on the other hand, I faked them all... And I faked them well.

Still, My soul needed some restoration. Some signs that it exists. With my feelings lost in the Oblivion, I had to think of something. The one thing I could think of... Pain. The only constant good thing in my life.

That's the thing about pain... It never leaves. I began the process of forcing my body into believing that it was in pain. How? By putting my body in the ways of harm. By punching whatever I could find. Mostly Walls and Doors. Hoping one day, There'll be a head instead of a brick.

The sight of blood... Set my teeth on edge, always. Ironical, eh? My philosophy had started differing by now. I had Crimson blood... Enough to get by as a human. It helped me control the chaos, that was my Mind.

By now, I had gotten success in convincing the society that I was doing fine. Outside, I was charming... Still am. Inside... I was a mess... Not anymore, though.

The Trauma that my health was going through after putting my body through all that... It wasn't gone. It's still hasn't and It never will. A wise man had once said... If you can't beat your demons, Join them. That's exactly what I did.

Instead of basking in their Grievance, I admired them with all my glory. Their will to get ahead of everyone... Their spark of standing tall at the end of the day and Most of all... Their ability to enjoy the chaos in pain.

I was a part of them and I enjoyed it. I enjoyed their company, I cherished their teachings. They taught me the value of perseverance. The value of getting back up. The value of being human. The value of having emotions, Real ones.

Hereafter, They lived happily after. Not really. There were times when I let my demons get the better of me. When I let them free... In the world out there, The Cruel world. A world where they want to reign and that's the only thing that kept me from becoming a Demon, myself.

The want to prove. The want to reign the world and The desire of never ever letting my family down.

One Morning... I woke up. I took a look outside. I stared at the sun in a hope that I'd be burned. It's glazing sunlight teared through my eyes... Making me screech in suffering. I had never felt pain in that manner before. Why now? Were my emotions back? To my sheer craving... They were not... But There was hope. Hope that one day, They'll be there.

That hope is still driving me. That hope is still able to grasp me and protect me from the weary hands of Lunacy.

That's all it took for me to get back my life.... Hope.

Priyankaa Padhi

Priyankaa Padhi is currently pursuing her Bachelors in Pharmacy from Roland Institute of Pharmaceutical sciences, Berhampur. She hails from Rourkela, Odisha. She is a passionate Orator, writer and an aesthete. She is a trained Indian classical singer. She believes in the power of the Universe and smart work to achieve anything and everything!

BIRDIE & THE FALL....!!!!

Birdie, birdie once on that tree!
With every detachment of the foliage,
Did you scrutinize anything?
The mighty winds have snatched-
away the lush green scenes.
With every fall,
An unhackneyed life was born,
The senile treasures were lost,
Flowers kept dreaming for blossoms,
Sunshine over the globe has faded.
Darkness has become prominent.
Tanning and sunburns were no concerns,
The cirpings of birdies have silenced,
The conspicuous, fluttering flight
of the butterflies were once seen.
The meadows & the feilds have vanished,
The vaults of the sky seems to be despondent,
It has started lacking it's charisma.
Everything else seems to be dull & dusty.
The spiderwaves were difficult to handle,
Meanwhile the frost is wraggling ,
Singing a welcome jingle!
Birdie birdie once on that tree,
With every detachment of the foliage,
Did you scrutinize anything ?
Man has changed,
Conflicting with his mood swings,
Ravishing for the harvest,
But melancholy for the dullness,
But trust me ,O birdie!
The universe is all about break & create,
One must fall to rise back !

Phalguni Jagadeesh

I am Phalguni Jagadeesh. I have completed my masters and also have worked for sometime in an outsourcing company as an Associate Recruiter.

Writing is my passion from young age which I will never stop doing. Now I have got a great platform to showcase my talent. I am also improving my skill because I am not a professional poet or a writer. I keep my words simple and just weave my thoughts.

A budding writer and has seven anthologies already published and few more yet to be published. A happy soul, finding peace and myself through writing.

"Not ashamed" is not just an anthology. It just doesn't have poems or stories, it has messages and motivational lessons for the people to improve their or others' mental health. Because not only physical health is needed to be taken care of, even mental health is to be taken care of. In fact, mental health issues needs more care and more importantly it needs more love to cure than the physical issues.

Depression is a phase like the black clouds. Once if it rains, sky will be clear.

New version

Shattered dreams,
Scattered life,
Troubled from inside,
Didn't know how to express.
Locked inside her room.

Tried to collect the pieces,
Never wanted to wake up,
No idea what to do next,
Locked up, shut everyone out,
Silence filled around, bothered her mind.

Needed a shoulder to lean,
None would understand, she knew.
Cried till tears dried up,
Trying to figure out things,
But, burdened mind never let her.

Luckily got a hand,
Came out of darkness,
Yet people called her mad.
Stayed calm, did what she wanted,
Swayed with new version of her.

©phal_candy

"Anxiety doesn't hurt me anymore. Body shaming or bullying is my sword to kill anxiety."

Courageous empress

"Ugly duckling"
"Fatty ass"
Were the names she got.
Cornered everyday like a mannequin,
Body shaming toy she became.

Awful comments were passed,
Cat called every time,
Anxiety killed her.
She couldn't handle anymore,
Hated herself the way she was.

Hid herself wherever she went,
Tortured was her life.
Until one day,
Trying to overcome her anxiety,
Flaunting her flaws,

Bold and brave she faced people,
Not ashamed any more,
Became an inspiration to many,
Even to the one's who taunted her.
Courageous empress she became.

©phal_candy

"OCD - Obsessive Complusive Disorder turned to be Obsessive Careful Deal. Not ashamed to frame my mental illness."

Picture perfect

Everyone called him rude.
"Aggressively behaving personality"
Tagged with this name,
He couldn't handle.

He wanted people to be clean.
He wanted things to be perfect.
Adopted a policy, "Just right"
Even without his knowledge.

Photography was his everything.
He needed things to be perfectly aligned
Else he would rage out,
The only problem he had, which was uncontrollable.

Gradually understood his OCD,
He made it his strength.
Clicked pictures even though it was asymmetrical,
Which walked him towards success.

OCD remained the same,
But, pictures came out excellent.
World famous photographer he became.
Carried his fame and OCD all together to his success.

©phal_candy

Shafia khanam

Shafia khanam was born and raised in Bhopal, India. She is a nineteen year old college student pursuing her bachelor's degree in engineering. She's often seen getting scoldings from her parents for scribbling poems and stories on her notebooks everytime she sits to study. She's a pesky sister to three of her siblings. Often perplexed by what next, she lets go of her worries by sketching hilarious sketches and finding solace in amateur metaphors.

She gets her inspiration from her grandmother who's an indomitable spirit defying all odds teaching her ways to survive this harsh world, saying i did, you can too. She feeds herself with these beautiful old memories her grandmother tells her about.

Apart from spending her time playing with electric circuits and wires, she loves visiting libraries rather than living in reality. She likes going on dates with Kahlil Gibran, Paulo Coelho, John Green to name a few.

She aims to make her parents proud someday. Paper and pen being her best friends, she scribbles a lot smelling the aroma of hot coffee spreading all over the room till the shutters of eye permits her to. She's often burdened with too little to do, so she just writes a lot.

DANK DUSK

Days are cold, nights even colder
The world's huddling behind warm blankets
And for you it's just bare skin, struggling within is the blood spurning to escort the course reaching the heart
Which already is brimmed and at this point has lost it's strength to endure further

The skies drenched you with rains of sorrows
And you, drained your eyes with solute of water and solvents of pain
You watch the skies changing colours at a pace so fast,
Leaving you perplexed which shade to trust for it brought you the sun and left you with storms

But then, there's hope, and somewhere we know the mist would clear up, not anytime sooner, but it will
And the sun will bring with it it's warmth
And with it will follow the spring, blooming new flowers and bringing scents of gaiety

But winter will make a visit too, like it's now, like it had before
Only to make you stronger from what you were yesterday
And one day you'll need no blankets or steaming teas to keep you warm,
Because it had already made you stronger to an extent that now this warrior needs no armour

And maybe, today is that day.
And if not today, i hope it would be tomorrow.

-Shafia Khanam

BUOYANT

When mist of doubts encircle your mind
And fighting doesn't seems an easy choice

When darkness seems to be a never ending ride
And no one really can hear your voice

When the world is wrapped in beautiful joys
And you only have loneliness by your side

When besieged with monsters every night
And you have your own demons to fight

When cold has shivered your body
And it had been long since your hope has died

Darling,
I assure you
The sun's waiting on the other side.

- Shafia Khanam

OKAY NOT OKAY

It ain't a shame
And i agree I'm in pain
Tired of plastering fake smiles
When I'm hiding hundreds of plights
You come and ask me,
How are you and are things going fine
I wonder how you can't see those suffering in my eyes
And did my OKAY ever sufficed?
I need one pat, but please don't tell me
Everything's gonna be fine
I have seen days more worst
But, fighting alone everytime is what hurts
Crying my problems out, for that I've no guts
For sympathy, I've no intention
But i know if you'll listen, it will reduce half of my tension
So next time you see anyone with weary eyes
It might be a case they have cried the whole night
Don't say, everything will be alright
Just give them a hug
And say, I'm here for you,
Come let's make it whole again, my bub.

- Shafia Khanam

Misha Garg

Misha Garg,also known as 'redstrings' is a hardcore Punjabi girl who lives in the city of Patiala. She is a self proclaimed bookworm and an awesome cook. She can be often seen roaming around in the halls of her University library or rummaging through the shelves of stores for a new recipe or ingredient to try out. She is currently pursuing her graduation in the field of commerce and she has a weird fascination with the sound of her fingers tapping on keys of a calculator. She is cheerful by nature, but is prone to extreme mood swings when hungry . She writes to escape her mind yet always ends up exploring herself .She loves watching Slice of Life animation works by Japanese companies . Her current favourite is "Barakamon". She is tone deaf but has a penchant for exploring new genres of music to soothe her ears.

Depression

What do they say
In bent whispers of gray
Taunting thee in stinging sway
Of reckless screams on stolen way
Some monsters eating out on a lonely day
Dunking morsels in dip of nightmares in tray
Opening ledgers of prey in guise of mere night play
Totalling debts owed to eyes with a silent death in bay
Some caged fears ask who told thee tears dont slay ?
Selling out thee cries with a blank cheque as pay
Tail of snake cries to ghosts in a marble cave
Who told thee that tongue doesnt slay ?
Thou mind is in an endless replay
Butchering in your own grave

"There are some screaming tears
lying under my lone fear
frozen by death of heart, hung on spear
of words my shadows whisper
corroding my dreams for death, they wear."

Chatter banter hustles in halls,
Pitter patter rustles on doors,
Laughing faces move along floors,
But i lay still covered and bored.
Gazing at distance, just closing on walls.
Scratching, but never opening those doors!
Bleeding hopes, my dreams nevermore.
Talking at lengths, blues steal my soul.
Shouting under pillows, my demons probe,
Guilty I am of murder of my own, still you ask whats wrong?
When i look outside, world hides its shore,
Drowning smiles, in endless depths i dont even care to mourn.
Sinking and sinking ,too deep and too far , i let go of my last roar,
Tired of washing away my tears once again in downpour.
Mirror whispers, songs of a loser, whining on streets selling her core.
Being bought on dimes are slanders, once again pain was whats left in store.
Still the world wonders what exactly has gone wrong?

Yes , Mental Abuse is lethal !!

"Easy to pour upon my starving lungs
Venom to gouge out my dying tongue
Smoke to smother on my bleeding eyes
Fire to be burned out of my crying heart
Rust to pile upon my wrangling limbs
Guilt to force upon my screaming ears
Rumors to paint black my forsook tears"

Flowers burned in million thoughts,
Stems reaching heavens were cut short,
Leaves transpired tears hidden in pot,
Morsels of leftover fruits decayed in rot,
Clinging to tendrils snail moves on slope,
Each step in stealth to entrap despair in corpse.

Living on breaths bones pulled back flesh,
When did her feet , slipped off from sledge!
Ice exhumed frozen fears sleeping in nest,
Covered by feathers of ruth a heart, mere pest.

Yelling cicadas drowned all parables taught,
Ringing in ears they welcomed senses drought,
When did she let go of all sorrows she bought?
Frolicking in market shopping million of thoughts,
Or catching onto mulish despair hanging from her boat .

Ahsanat Chaudhary

Ahsanat Chaudhary is a budding writer, precisian, solitudinarian at times and holds a post graduate degree in English literature. A graduate degree in management studies has helped her polish various aspects of writing. Being an enthusiastic educator, she believes to write for change so that the world could be a better place to breathe in. She sometimes has an appalling and almost irresistible urge to eat nachos at midnight.

Thief by default.

Stealing the hung chandelier,
Carefree strolling, barefoot.
Silence languidly gripping me,
I was walking past the wood.
Craving for warmth.
The lonely long winter,
Vitiated my corrupt soul.
I felt a confluent lacuna,
Wintry desolation surrounded me.
I kept walking with tepid steps.
Void of warmth engulfing me.
I could hear the silence sing.
Yodelling morbid melancholy with every pace.
Uncanny sinister shadows, loomed in front of me.
I leapt and run through the cobblestones streets.
A lopsided snowman stood right in front of me.
I felt my stars gleamed a little more.
I hugged it, embracing all the warmth it had.
"Don't! It's not yours", an anonymous voice whispered.
I mocked and grabbed it as if it was mine.
In the collection of stolen souvenirs, my snowman would enshrine.

(Topic touched-Kleptomania)

Eternal hope.

An unforeseen episode,
Took her darling away.
Her chest explodes.
Shattering every day.
Daily she dies,
In bits and fragments.
She still hears his voice.
Undying sentiments.
His smell still lingers.
On bedsheets, wrinkled and soiled.
His touch still sinks her.
Burying in the grave unspoiled.
She is nothing but a living carcass.
Disintegrating swiftly in delusion.
Her life is an interminable darkness.
Recurrent terrifying hallucinations.
From murky dawn to wintry night fall,
Its for him her heart craves.
For solace, her feet daily crawl,
To his grave for comforting embrace.

(Topic touched - Psychosis)

Unquenchable fire.

I love my fire.
Eternal and hostile.
Kindle, enkindle.
Strong and vile.
I am the fuel for it.

I saw the Bonfire.
With flames, brilliant bright.
I felt so ecstatic.
It felt so right.
My heart is an inferno.

I felt terribly low.
I saw a matchstick lying there.
I burned the closet.
Watched it with hypnotic stares.
Fireworks set off all over my soul.

(Topic touched - Pyromania)

L

G

B

T

Let's Grow and Bloom Together

Aashna Aga

LET "SHE" BE "FREE"

All rights are reserved for boys,
While girls have no rights to raise their voice,
No hurdle for boys, it's only for girls,
Boys have freedom, while in trap of rights are girls,
Why sex difference?
Why suffering for women's?
Respiring same air, color of blood is same,
Then why rules and rights, as if life is game,
Don't kill emotions, don't let feelings die,
Let every human be free,
Let every human fly....
©queen_of_words_ashu

THE BOND CALLED "TOGETHERNESS"

Black are treated based on their skin tone,
By fair skin people holding heart of stone,
Poor have special place, somewhere in gloom,
While rich have reservation to bloom,
This is what the real meaning of "Rights"?
This is what the real meaning of "equality"?
Where is the meaning of "Togetherness" is lost?
To earn happiness human being have to pay cost,
Why only importance to money but value feelings too,
And show the humanity within you,
Understand the poor soul, encourage them to grow,
Let the zephyr of unity and pride blow,
Let's share together....
Let's bloom together....
Let's grow together....
©queen_of_words_ashu

LET'S OVERTHROW ENMITY

If she is female she can't go out at night,
If she is lady for herself she alone can't fight,
He is a man and he is great and strong,
And if woman try to clash with him, then it's wrong,
Why vast place for discrimination but why not for love?
Why vast place for discernment but why not for love?
Sex, age, colour , language based discrimination,
Are welcoming more and more complications,
Mentor the one who is in need,
Helpless soul you try to feed,
Even enlightened many forget the meaning of education,
Such are those cruel human who much believe in
discrimination,
Instead of getting embroiled, find ways to annihilate it,
So that no more emotional burden life have to greet...
©queen_of_words_ashu

Aarthi Sampath

I am Aarthi Sampath, Artist based in Chennai, 37 yr old, I have muscular Dystrophy and I use wheelchair,Pet lover,Painting was my profession,

But now I am a writer, I have written lots of articles about me, and I write to break stigma, against bullies, about self-love self-aware

I'm a co author of Anthologies "clipped wings grow", "Letters to self","Untold, Unwritten Unheard", Hashtag "#metoo"

"clipped wings glow"

which has been published, and some more upcoming anthologies too.

I am Thankful for Kalon Maple Publishing

And Mrunaal Gawhande And Komal

For these excellent Anthologies and for Encouraging Writers Like me. And I am Glad to join this team My motto

"Write what you witness that "witnessed your existence"

Pride

In every pulse there's a Love
Throbbing with desires
Longing to breathe under our skin
And in our coral seas there's a song
Unheard, coursing through our veins
In every pulse there's a pride
Kissing our lips until we die,
And our hands intertwined
Irrespective of the genders our body holds,Love blooms like wildflowers
Uninterruptedly,
Everyday, Everywhere, and in Everything
And redolent of Love is too intense
to be abhorred
And we are not here to be hated
But to Live and breathe equality
And shoulder to shoulder we stood
In the endless nights of yesterdays
to earn our choices to live the way we want, to share our lives the way we wanted
And We are here now Wrapped into the skins of tomorrows
embracing the liberty to love without being judged.

Love Carnation

The earth is a bowl of carnation
Mostly we were named deep reds,
pink and purple
It's been our signature for ages
We blossomed, We Rise, We have a soul deep rooted,
We've been celebrated for who we are,
We may wither but not fade
For we were bequeathed, that even our bones blossom,
Soul to Soul
Flesh to Flesh
Skin to Skin,
Lips to Lips
Woman to Woman
Man to Man
We share a Bond,
We have tales of ecstasy
We want to be heard
Cause we are rare to be caged in our ribs, and our flutters never cease
As Love can't be trapped in a closet
We want to Love and not to be labelled for whom we love to l ive with And we will unabashedly kiss our privileges of being human
Cause we are Bunch of Carnations
Born to take pride.

Unapologetically Gay

Love is Raw, a feeling beyond discrimination,
Love is not about gender or skin colour
It doesn't need approval
It's your body and soul responding to same sex or non-binary
t's about acknowledging your body
It's about the box of needs
You carry in you, to be seen and felt
As who you're
It's about being human
It's about living
with someone who you could share everything comfortably
And just like that, you fall in love,
Like nothing really matters,
everybody yaps about sins
If you're so much Gay
or you're a non-binary and
If that doesn't match their social, cultural ethics
then you would be blamed for loving
or marrying man to man, woman to woman, or others
But you dare not change the way you're, Because someday
when they break the walls down
You would be written in the history for being Unapologetically
Gay.

Ahsanat Chaudhary

Ahsanat Chaudhary is a budding writer, precisian, solitudinarian at times and holds a post graduate degree in English literature. A graduate degree in management studies has helped her polish various aspects of writing. Being an enthusiastic educator, she believes to write for change so that the world could be a better place to breathe in. She sometimes has an appalling and almost irresistible urge to eat nachos at midnight.

Belongingness.

Waging war against the societal norms.
Coming out amidst the hurricane and storms.

In a world which is not meant for my existence.
I try to fit in with untiring and constant persistence.

Constructed notions of beauty haunt me to the core.
I feel like an ill fitted garment, always ignored.

I am not a man of muscles; I have innumerable hesitations.
Mainstream gay culture has toxic expectations.

The plethora of labels, the race of being a normate guy.
Too fat, too fem, too slim, these names why?

I diet and starve, struggle to be accepted by my peers.
But daily in the club I have no one to cheer.

These constant rejections make me question my identity.
Are these ideal beauty standards more than a person's sanctity?

I choose to live with my deepest truth, but I will not change anymore.
I may not be the glamor guy; these beauty standards are hollow to the core.

Its time that we re-examine our culture and build a community strong.
I would now stop to fit in because LGBT is where I belong.

Don't label me.

Gender.
Complicated, multi-layered.
Ongoing process, hiding, outing.
Equal status seems just a dream.
Human.

Identity.
Bicurious, agender.
Closeted, coming out, demi romantic.
The struggle is never ending.
Human.

Two spirits.
Transvestite, transsexual.
Transitioning, withering, questioning.
The conflict continues.
Human.

Gender binary.
Rigid, Compulsive.
Prohibiting, unaccepting, condemning.
Perpetual pain lingers.
Human.
(Topic touched-Unwanted labels)
Multiple Didactic cinquain.

Flag of pride.

Celebrating pride.
Embracing diversity.
Splendid India.

Flag of pride flutter.
Life blushing dark scarlet red.
Orangish healing.

Tinged with yellow hues,
Chromatic verdant lush green,
Wrapping nature.

Gentle harmony,
Prevailing through the blue band.
Purple spirit soars.

Diversity smiles.
Individualism thrives.
Love, live and let live.

(Topic touched-Acceptance in India)
Multiple haiku.

#not_ashamed

Dibyadarshini Behera

We say it's wrong
and against the nature
We called them horrid things,
when will u mature...

We act as though we choose this,
like they asked for hate,
This is just how they were born,
that is their fate...

Don't hate because they are ifferent
As that still up to you
In fact you should proud be of them
For they come out to you!!

When we can not stop the roar of oceans
Then how can we stop their emotions
Boys can like pink, girl can wear blue
Your reflection is up to you

#not_ashamed

We accept it or not
They still roam in this earth
They are only wanted to fit in
So why??
we are so hateful towards them from birth!!

Debjeet Mukherjee

As of 2018, Debjeet Mukherjee is a post graduate student of economics at the University of Calcutta. His first short story "A Rural Coincidence", won a Commendable Mention at the Wingword Short Story Prize 2017 organized by Delhi Poetry Slam. He was Shortlisted the following year, for his internationally acclaimed story "The Farewell", at the Wordweavers India Short Story 2018 Contest. These short story booklets, self-published in 2019 by Uditi Prakashan, helped Mukherjee establish himself as an author with a promising future. Mukherjee also received an Honorable Mention for his winning entry "Two Birds", at the International Photography Awards 2017 under Non-Pro Nature - Wildlife category.

Debjeet Mukherjee's debut international poetry book "VOYAGES Volume I – A Collection of Poetry", self-published in 2018 / deluxe edition in 2019 by Notion Press, was reviewed and rated Five Stars by Readers' Favorite, USA and Realistic Poetry International. The poetry collection was bestowed a (Four Stars) Silver Book Award by Literary Titan, USA in February 2019 and garnered favorable positive feedback from authors, bloggers and reviewers around the world. The book also received a Gold Star in TheBookDesigner.com's September 2018 e-Book Cover Design Awards. The official website of the author is www.debjeetmukherjee.com

Society of Dreams

I've seen her laugh in silence,
Amidst clouds of hope
That one day, she can love
Her best friend of late.

I've seen him scorn the mass,
Who laughed, while he
Held hands and walked to gym.
His partner, looking down shy.

People doubt us, don't believe us.
We stare at genders alike.
I mean no harm, just my taste;
Willing to endure my fate.

I did not choose this life.
I was not born this way.
A promise was made for living,
The heavens stand as witness.

Time heals everything.
I believe it, more so now.
But will time give back moments?
Moments lost, in convincing them?

Manali Debroy

Rainbow

Colours of love -
They marinate the soul with compassion.
With tenderness of the heart,
we accept other souls into our lives,
like our own umbra.
If love is the colour of life,
then why discriminate it with gender?
If love is pure and true,
then why hide it like a crime?
And if love is heavenly,
then why punish like it's something infernal?
Why not celebrate colours of love unanimously?
Why paint just a biased love story,
when we can paint a rainbow,
and celebrate colours with every loved soul!

- by Manali Debroy

www.ingramcontent.com/pod-product-compliance
Lightning Source LLC
LaVergne TN
LVHW091557170726
843492LV00007B/2175

* 9 7 8 8 1 9 4 7 6 3 4 9 9 *